ASK-BELIEVE-RECEIVE

A DIVINE GIFT

A GUIDE TO MANIFESTING
LOVE AND ALL YOU
DESIRE THROUGH THE
LAW OF ATTRACTION

BY

ANNE LAUREN

The content of this book contains the author's research and personal experiences. The author does not claim to be a physician, psychologist or mental health professional or dispense any medical advice. The reader should seek treatment for any emotional issues before beginning to improve their life through The Law of Attraction *Principles, Processes and Components.* The author cannot guarantee, that if you study and use the material in this book, you will attain your goal to manifest or improve your life for the better. The intent of the author is to teach you The Law of Attraction information, and to help you in your quest for spiritual growth and wellbeing.

Book Cover by Anne Lauren

ISBN: 978-1-951188-68-9
Library of Congress Control Number: 2022921480

Published by Hallard Press LLC.
www.HallardPress.com
Bulk copies of this book can be ordered at
Info@HallardPress.com

Dedication

This book is dedicated to my late dad, David Warschauer, who passed away when I was just 1 ½ years old. He was a book author and a music composer. As I was writing this book I felt he was dictating words and spiritual information through me, from the heavenly realm. As my fingers swiftly tapped the computer keys, I sometimes had to stop and look up word definitions that were unfamiliar to me.

I want to thank Barry Fuss, (Bear) who is a warm, lovable, huggable soul who introduced me to his Law of Attraction groups at the "bear den". I would never be where I am today if it wasn't for his support and guidance.

I am thankful and grateful to God and the universal energies for my one and only twin flame who I met at the perfect time and place. It took three years to finally manifest him and if it were not for my strong determination and patience to never give up, I would not have met him in this lifetime. He was the catalyst to writing this book and we have had over eight wonderful years together.

From this day forward, I dedicate this book to all the present and future enlightened souls who are ready to change their life for the better.

Contents

PART IV THE FIFTH DIMENSION

Introduction

"You want to become aware of your thoughts, you want to choose your thoughts carefully and you want to have fun with this, because you are the masterpiece of your own life."

Joe Vitale

The Law of Attraction is the most amazing law in the universe when used in a positive way. Being able to manifest anything you want, through your thoughts and intentions, is one of the greatest feelings you could ever have in your life. These amazing manifestations do not just happen by coincidence, luck, magic, or fate, they only happen through The Law of Attraction in action! The title, "*A Divine Gift*", fits perfectly with the subject matter because, every positive manifestation is a gift from *a* divine source.

Children have an expansive imagination and enjoy creating something out of nothing. Even though they are not taught The Law of Attraction, they have an innate ability to manifest whatever they desire just by making a wish, asking for what they want, and believing they will receive it. When I was a young child I had no idea about The Law of Attraction. But, all my wishes were granted when I would ask for and visualize what I wanted while blowing out birthday candles or throwing a penny into a fountain.

Later in life I had some trying times. My marriage was falling apart, my health was not good, and I was depressed and unhappy. I could not manifest anything but negative situations and I didn't know how to get out of my funk. One of my friends gave me The Law of Attraction movie entitled, *"The Secret"*, by Rhonda Byne. After watching the movie, I realized that I had to raise my mood from despair and depression to love, joy, and happiness in order to manifest all good things into my life. I also learned that I had freewill to choose what I wanted to believe as well as, how I wanted to feel each minute of every day.

Most adults don't trust their inner knowledge and have lost the ability to create their own life experiences. They believe that whatever happens is either considered good luck or bad luck and have no control over how things turn out. But, we do have control, as the book, The Course in Miracles states, *"Anything that you truly desire, with your whole being, you will experience."* The Bible states, *"If you ask it will be given to you. Every door will be opened to you."*

Learning to manifest is like a recipe that has many important ingredients, and if you leave out any of The Law of Attraction *Principles, Processes and Components,* you will not be able to manifest what you desire.

THE PRINCIPLES are very important and you must learn to do the following before you can continue on to the *Processes and Components*:

- Clear out any negativity in your life.
- Change negative beliefs and replace them with positive, new beliefs.
- Love yourself.
- Become more spiritual.
- Understand vibrational energy, dimensions and the Universal Laws as they relate to manifesting.

THE PROCESSES are the basis to manifesting what you desire:

- ***Ask*** for what you want, by way of your *Letter of Intention* and *Vision Board.*
- ***Believe*** that what you desire will manifest.
- ***Receive*** your *divine gifts* through *your Inner Guidance System,* at the perfect universal time and place.

THE COMPONENTS are the instructions on how to manifest. You cannot have one without the other otherwise, you will have difficulty manifesting. They are as follows:

- ***Meditation*** - Will clear and relax your mind so as to visualize your desires.

- ***Vision Board*** - A large poster board where you will cut out and tape pictures of what you want to manifest, visualizing them as if you already have what you desire.

- ***Letter of Intention*** - Is your written letter to God or whomever you pray to, describing in detail, what you desire.

- ***Inner Guidance System*** - Is an inner voice within your mind, like *a* GPS, that directs you to when and where you will receive your *divine gifts*. You must learn to be aware of this very important *Component* otherwise, you will miss your opportunity to receive what you have asked for.

- ***Mood Ascension Scale*** - Is a personal scale of your current mood. It ranges from the highest 5th dimensional, vibrational frequency such as love, joy and happiness, to the lowest 3rd dimensional, vibrational frequency such as fear, anger and depression.

Manifesting is very simple and fun as well. The hardest part is to make the commitment to study the material and believe 100% it will work. If you are new to the Law of Attraction you need to be patient, take your time and do not rush through the book. Once you understand and use the *Principles, Processes and Components,* you will have the confidence to begin to manifest parking spaces. At this point, you will feel an amazing wellbeing in your life as The Law of Attraction takes form. Just try to have an open mind and absorb whatever rings true to you.

As you follow the information in the first six chapters you will begin to change your life for the better, and it will be a positive step in the right direction. This book is only your guide, and I cannot guarantee your success, it is up to you to make it all happen.

This is the first day of the rest of your life. Don't waste any more time mulling over the past, and what you don't have or the bad situations you are presently experiencing. Have fun with the Law of Attraction and remember to:

ENJOY LIFE - BE HAPPY - LAUGH OFTEN - LOVE ALWAYS,

Anne Lauren

PART I

THE PRINCIPLES

"Shallow people believe in luck and real truth, seekers believe in The Law of Attraction."

Ralph Waldo Emerson

Chapter 1

Changing Your Life and Beliefs

"*The secret to having it all is believing that you have it all.*"

Changing Your Life:

If you have a burning desire to get whatever you want in your current and future life, and are willing to put effort and energy into changing yourself, then you are ready to begin this amazing journey. Getting your life in order is first and foremost before you can manifest your *divine gifts,* and begin to feel love, joy and happiness. You need to weed the garden of your heart, body and mind of all the negativity that you have been carrying around.

Pick the following activities that you want to change and add anything else that is not on the list. Take one at a time until you are satisfied with the results then go on to the next. You need to be patient with yourself, this is not a race.

- Redecorate your living space by painting rooms and old furniture.

- Clean out closets, cabinets and drawers.

- Buy new towels and sheets.

- Make your home environment comfortable and attractive.

- Replace any home furnishings that are either worn or broken.

- Spend time outdoors and plant flowers to add color to beautify your garden, patio or balcony. When your flowers bloom, butterflies and birds will appear, and it will give you a feeling that nature is always in harmony.

- Change your looks by getting a new hairstyle or haircut.

- Buy some new clothes and rid your closet of what you do not wear or the items you no longer need. Donate them to charity or have a garage sale and make some pocket money.

- Eat healthy foods by growing an organic vegetable garden that will be fun to tend to each day.

- If you are creative learn to write a book or paint a picture.

- Get more exercise that will strengthen your body and relax your mind as you learn a dance routine, workout at a gym, ride a bike or take a walk.

- To stimulate your mind, join The Law of Attraction study groups. This is where you will find many likeminded seekers and possibly make some new friends.

- Get at least eight hours of sleep for more energy and vitality.

- Forgive any past loves and relationship where there was hurt, anger and or betrayal. Write their name(s) on a piece of paper, put them in a metal bucket and burn them outside. The smoke will remind you that your past has disappeared and is no longer in your heart and mind.

- Become someone who will attract positive situations and people into your new life, maybe even a new love interest.

- Visualize positive situations and outcomes. Disregard thoughts related to giving up, failures or roadblocks.

- Look for solutions rather than dwelling on your problems.

- Dissipate negative situations with love, compassion and understanding. If that does not work, just know that you cannot control conditions, persons, or things, you can only control your own thoughts and feelings.

- Change how you want to be treated by surrounding yourself with people who love you unconditionally and treat you with kindness.

- Every day feel gratitude for your blessings, both large and small.

- Have faith that you are connected to a higher power, and are one with this power, that will give you strength to attain anything and everything you want in your current lifetime.

- Don't get discouraged when you make a change in your life and run into obstacles, just know you are making progress and moving ahead.

Changing Your Beliefs:

There are people who are unhappy, stuck in a comfort mode and don't know how to get unstuck. They feel that they must "buy into the system" because that is what they have grown up to believe. If this sounds like you and, you want to make good things happen, you must decide to "step out of the box." Try new adventures instead of staying in your old habits that are not working for you. Successful people who had a dream never gave up, even when they had failure after failure.

Knowing what you want and what you do not want is called *contrast.* Whatever you believe is what you will manifest, be it either positive or negative, and can shape your life, drive you towards success and happiness, or failure and distress.

You have immediate access to an unlimited amount of whatever it is you want by believing in abundance instead of lack. In the universe there is no such thing as lack. When you focus on lack or what you don't have, be it love, money, happiness, etc. it does not feel good and will be a perpetual situation.

Be aware that you can either laugh or cry, feel happy or sad, strong or scared just by how you process any situation you experience. How you think and feel can have a profound effect on your ability to recognize opportunity, how well you perform and the outcome of the goals that you set for yourself.

We all must go through difficulties and heartache to learn lessons for soul growth, and is all part of the life process. In order to change your life you need to have the desire and be in a positive mode. Otherwise, nothing good will manifest and you will become discouraged. If you need some help with your problems or negativity, talk to a trusted friend, relative or mental health professional.

NOTES

Chapter 2

Loving Yourself, Human Love, And Divine Love

"When love is what we are born with, fear is what we learn. The spiritual journey is the unlearning of fear and the acceptance of love back into our hearts."

Marianne Williamson

In 1956, psychologist and social philosopher Erich Fromm, proposed two quotes, *"That loving oneself is different from being arrogant, conceited or egocentric." "Loving oneself means caring about, knowing oneself and taking responsibility (e.g. being realistic and honest about one's strengths and weaknesses.)*

There are two kinds of love, *human love and divine love.* The difference between the two is that *human or personal love,* is often conditional while *divine love or spiritual love* is unconditional. Divine love is the force that connects us all and is the essence of the divine. Through divine love you are connected to everything and everyone as well as, you are connected to the universal energy. Divine love is from the soul, as opposed from the human ego or personality. The more ego that is involved the less harmonious your relationships will be. Immature love means, I love you because I need you. Mature love means, I need you because I love you.

Often in *human love,* there are possessiveness, demands or expectations that are all based on conditions, limitations, or material and selfish desires. Because of a feeling of lack, human love often seeks outside oneself when the person is looking for someone to fill a void within their empty heart. With divine love, there is no need to possess or control each other.

In a soulmate relationship, that is just based on conditional love, as in sexual lust or obsessive love, a person will be going through this revolving door many times for soul growth. When these lessons have finally been learned, and energy, thoughts, and vibrations shift to a higher 5D, unconditional divine love, then a person can manifest their twin flame all in perfect universal timing.

Love must come solely from your state of being and can only begin inside you. It is your natural longing in life to experience this depth of love, especially when you are with your twin flame. As we grow we gain wisdom and boundaries to discern what love truly is and what it isn't. Love is all there is and the highest 5D, vibrational energy in the universe. It is a powerful force and through love anything is possible. It is not found by looking for love out there but, by going within to find self-love and radiating that love around.

If you are looking for romantic love through social networks, internet dating sites, fix ups, bars, and dances, you will find many romantic soulmates, some great and some not so great. You want to be in love so much that when a potential mate does come along, you feel this could be your one and only true love. But, no one is going to make you happy, fill in your missing parts, give you the love you need and want so much, as well as solve all your issues. If this person leaves the relationship, through death or other reasons, you would probably feel a deep void. It is impossible to give love to another from a place of fear and lack, as this comes from being desperate for love to be returned.

Only you can give love to someone else when you are already overflowing with self-love. As you love and accept yourself exactly as you are, it makes it easier to go through the so-called difficult times. The relationship between you, your higher self, and the universal energies will absolutely influence every single relationship you will ever have. Your connection to yourself is the connection you form with others and the process to manifestation through The Law of Attraction.

Setting Boundaries for Self-love:

- Love, respect and care for yourself spiritually, emotionally, and physically before you can love someone else.

- Don't feel rejected when you speak your truth about what you believe in, and stay strong in what it is you stand for.

- When people demand something from you, create boundaries as to what you will and will not do.

- It is your choice to say "yes" or "no" when you feel something does, or does not suit you spiritually, emotionally or physically.

- Care for yourself and define whom you are as well as what you need. Take responsibility for yourself.

- Do not feel you need to apologize for your past, but live an authentic, regret free life in the present and future.

- You don't have to be perfect so don't be so hard on yourself. Just relax, honor your needs and feelings, do what makes you happy and enjoy life.

- Live in the present only, the past is gone and the future is for creating your new life through The Law of Attraction.

- Laugh more, worry less, and keep a positive outlook. In doing so, your positive energy, thoughts and vibrations will shift to a higher level, and you will be able to start manifesting all your desires.

Unconditional Love With Your Partner:

- Even if you don't agree with your partner you can still love and accept them. Acceptance is a powerful antidote to anger so make peace not war.

- An empathetic connection and positive emotions are the secret to good relationships. Try to put yourself in their shoes and feel their feelings.

- Connect to your partner with love rather than a lack or need.

- Be generous and kind with your partner and focus on their positive attributes rather than putting them down or pointing out their negative traits.

- Remember, your life must be loving, joyful and happy before you can love and care for your partner. Make yourself happy by creating more laughter in your relationship, "Laughter is the best Medicine."

NOTES

Chapter 3

The Soul, The Spirit and Reincarnation

"True love doesn't have a happy ending, true love doesn't have an ending."

Anonymous

The Soul was born and created from spirit and has a purpose of growing, and learning with many soulmates throughout incarnations. The physical body is a vehicle for the soul and the soul is our consciousness and expression for which we live and have out active life.

The Spirit is who you are as an individual, is eternal, exists prior to one's physical body, and is the absolute perfection of that being. We are not physical beings having a spiritual experience, but spiritual beings having a physical experience.The human spirit is the electricity that animates us and the spark of the God source that keeps us alive. The human mind is the hardware of the body and comprises the brain, perception and memory. Our personality is the software or personality unique to each of us.

As strange as it may sound, before we are born in a physical body, we choose some of the major experiences that we desire to have, we make soul level contracts with other souls called "soulmates". Challenging situations and relationships often are brought about by the greatest opportunities, for the individual to learn various life lessons, and to grow spiritually. At birth, aspects of your personality, character, talents, abilities, weaknesses and strengths are already formed in essence as part of your soul, acquired throughout lifetimes. That is why all newborns have their own personalities at birth and so do identical twins.

Reincarnation is not a religion but, a complicated system for souls to address their spiritual growth. It was a belief system before it was taken out of the bible in 553 AD. Thousands of years ago the Egyptians believed in the afterlife, and today reincarnation is going strong in the Hindu and Buddhist religions. The concept of reincarnation might seem foreign to some who do not believe we live more than just this lifetime. I would suggest for those who feel this way to keep an open mind, do research on this subject and take in what resonates within you. To others, it might seem natural that the soul has been born many lifetimes, especially when it refers to the spiritual journey of soulmates and twin flames.

Some people have a knowing about a specific place, lifestyle or type of work that seems very familiar to them and they feel it could be from past life experiences.

Remembering past lives can be difficult because we do not know much about who we were or where we lived. This is to experience each life fresh with a new perspective that is not influenced by a prior lifetime. We have had a history of many incarnations with our soulmates and twin flames. When we meet, there is an instant recognition that we have known this person before. If you have an interest in what type of past lives you have had you can have a past life regression by a professional who specializes in hypnosis.

Nature is perfect in all its splendor. There are seasons in the plant world where perennial flowers and trees die off in the winter and come back to life in the spring, spouting their new foliage for many years. This is how the creator designed the life cycle and we are no different. Nothing is random, everything is happening for a reason and we all have a purpose in life.

NOTES

Chapter 4

Spirituality, Vibrational Energy And Dimensions

"If you want to find the secrets of the universe, think in terms of energy, frequency and vibration."

Nikola Tesla

Spirituality is the search for the meaning of life. It is our natural way of being and is a sense of connection to something bigger than ourselves. It is a feeling that you are more than just your present situation, like your physical body, race, gender, family, job, and statues in life. You feel an intuitive perception of the causes behind conditions.

One of the main teachings of spirituality is to find what you are seeking within yourself and that you are eternal, timeless, and deeply profound. The Law of Attraction and spirituality work together and, in order for you to reach a higher vibrational frequency, you can't have one without the other. If you don't understand spirituality, as it applies to The Law of Attraction, the process will fail to work and positive manifestations will not happen. You can look up spirituality on the

the Internet if you do not understand the concept and want more information. Earth is a spiritual place filled with divine beings who are governed by love. Unfortunately, in today's world, humans have lost their way, and we are now living in a matrix of false interpretations of this love and spiritual reality. In order to be free of this matrix and be one with the universal energies, we need to begin to educate ourselves as to what is the true reality of spirituality. Also, we must ignore what is told to us through the media to cause fear and lose our sense of who we are within our spiritual core.

The world started with spirituality and all religions were born from this belief system. Religion and spirituality are not the same thing but they have some similarities. Religion is an organized group or culture that acts with a mission, with the intention of presenting specific teachings and a way of life. The core of religion is spirituality, and to improve one's emotional wellbeing one must seek a meaningful, profoundly powerful, spiritual connection to God and the universal energies.

This can result in positive feeling of contentment, gratitude, peace, awe and acceptance that we are in charge of ourselves and what happens in our lives. If you are religious, do not give up your present belief system as you learn and practice The Law of Attraction.

Your religious beliefs, combined with The Law of Attraction study and spirituality, will only enhance your life and make it so much better.

Vibrational Energy is a stream of wellbeing that never stops flowing through all living entities. In order for The Law of Attraction to work you must realign to this universal energy stream, and reclaim your innate power to create your own reality. We are all part of the universal source energy, call it whatever your beliefs are, and you can connect to it through meditation and prayer. You cannot resist or deny this energy or it won't work as you would like it to. You hinder your connection when you are in a state of resistance and nothing is working out for you.

Everything in the universe vibrates on a frequency of energy from an atom to the planets. Humans, insects, and animals can feel vibrational frequencies, and will respond positively or negatively to the environment they are surrounded by. Plants can feel positive vibrational energy and flourish or negative, vibrational energy, and will wither and/or die.

Everything that is experienced in the physical environment is vibration. Sounds vibrate throughout the ear canal to be able to hear, some being pleasant and some irritating. Smells, touch and taste all have either positive or negative vibrations. Words and emotions are the strongest vibrational feelings and gives a wealth of information, both pleasing and not so pleasing.

Whether we are vibrating on a lower, negative, vibrational frequency or a higher, positive, vibrational frequency, we will attract the same vibrational frequency. *"Like attracts like." "Every action creates an equal reaction." "What comes around, goes around."*

All thoughts match each other in vibration and when you offer a positive vibration of something that you desire, and put your attentions towards it, The Law of Attraction will give you what you ask for. But, when you say, "I hope, maybe, I don't believe, I am not sure, it's not possible," etc. you are then in a negative, vibrational thought pattern and it is guaranteed that what you want will be either delayed or will not manifest at all.

Solfeggio Tones are musical frequencies that can either raise your mood and make you feel happy, peaceful and joyful or lower your mood and make you feel uneasy, scared or anxious. Musical sounds and vibrations such as bells, chimes, meditation and classical music can help in a positive way with various aspects of body and mind health. Chaotic music, such as hard rock or heavy metal can put you in a negative mood and cause you to feel uncomfortable and irritated. Background music, in horror and war movies, can cause you to be fearful and anxious. It is important to be aware of what you listen to as it affects your whole being.

The Frozen Water Experiments on You Tube, by the scientist Dr. Masaru Emoto, explains how positive and negative sound wave, vibrational frequencies can affect water molecules when viewed under a microscope. He found that beautiful, snowflake designs appeared when there were positive, vibrational, frequency sound waves or words like, "*I love you, you are wonderful.*" were spoken. When sound wave molecules were exposed to negative, low vibrational, frequencies such as in heavy metal, hard rock music, or with words like, "*I hate you, you make me sick,*" the molecules became ugly, muted shapes.

We are made up of 70% water so just be aware that in order to feel happy and healthy, keep thinking positive thoughts and words. Listen to beautiful, relaxing music of your choice and your cells will love it!

Dimensions are many states of consciousness in which reality can exist all at the same time at different frequencies. There are many dimensions in the universe but, only the 3rd, 4th and 5th dimensional, vibrational, frequencies will be discussed here as it applies to The Law of Attraction. I will refer to them as 3D, 4D and 5D. The most common human dimension on earth is the 3D reality, where we have a strong awareness of being an individual with an ego, and a body that is separate from everyone else and all that is. These people have beliefs and self-identity that feel "normal" and focus on personal experiences and challenges, with little awareness of the higher, human 4D and 5D frequencies. The unenlightened person, who only lives in a lower 3D consciousness, will not know how to release themselves from this negativity until they awaken and are ready to learn and overcome their life lessons.

In 4D, we become aware that we are all part of the universal energy system and the Universal Law called "The Law of One." In this dimension we have complete control over what is happening in life instead of thinking everything is random in the 3D reality. In 4D, we can day dream and start creating whatever we want to manifest, especially in meditation or lucid dreaming. A person who is enlightened and open minded will be able to transcend from 3D to 4D and then to 5D at will.

There is only love, joy and happiness in 5D and it is where telepathy or unspoken words happen between twin flames. To ascend to 5D, manifest all you desire and unite with your twin flame, you must learn to love yourself and everyone else unconditionally. The Law of Attraction process works only if you believe 100%, that you can reach 5D and stay there, no matter what is going on around you. When you do, you will feel a sense of universal oneness and less individuality

You begin to meld with the divine, understand spiritual truth, and have feelings of power and control in your life. Your old ways of negative thinking will become obsolete, and you will never want to go back to living in the lower, dense, 3D vibrational frequency again. You will also begin to be aware of, and interact with human-like angelic beings, who will help you in your time of need.

The lowest, non-human dimensions are 1D and 2D. Generic rocks are 1D and simply exist without identity or self-awareness. Most mineral stones have a consciousness, such as quartz crystals, and can transmit positive energy for healing as well as transmit energy in watches and radios.

The mineral stone called amethyst, can also transmit positive energy and healing. Rose quartz crystals are aligned with the heart chakra and are used to encourage self-love and balancing of the heart energy. There are many other gemstones that vibrate at frequencies similar to the body chakras. If you have an interest to know more about the mineral stones and the chakras do your research on the Internet. You might want to buy some beautiful mineral stones to wear as jewelry to enhance your health and wellbeing.

Plants, animals, reptiles, fish, birds and insects have an innate consciousness and live in a 2D reality. They are all connected to the universal energies, and are aware of separation, duality, fear and polarity within their environment. Unlike humans, they do not have free will.

NOTES

Chapter 5

Universal Laws

"When working with the Universal Laws you are working with the laws of manifestation, not instant gratification."

Jennifer O'Neill

Our world is governed by Universal Laws originating in ancient Hawaiian culture. These laws need to be followed in order for harmony, joy and happiness to manifest in our lives. The following are just a few that correspond to The Laws of Attraction:

The Law of Attraction - This is the most recognized law in the universe, and states that we have the ability to attract anything into our reality depending on the vibrational energy that we are emitting as positive or negative. The more we align ourself with the vibration of what we are attracting, the more likely it is to manifest what we want or do not want. When we are in 5D, and believe 100% that our positive desires will manifest, we can attract the perfect opportunities and circumstances into our life.

The Law of Manifestation - Everything that we manifest, be it positive or negative, begins with a thought. We must create it in our mind before it manifests into our reality. The limits we put on ourself are the only things holding us back.

The Law of Expectation - Whatever we expect with certainty and confidence will become a self-fulfilling prophecy and will become our reality. Whether we are expecting a hard life or a life filled with opportunity, abundance, and divine gift*s,* it will be up to us. What we expect to receive will manifest both good and not so good. We can change our expectation at any time and it will manifest as we desire it.

The Law of Divine Oneness - We are all part of the grand web of life, and we have an important role to play in how reality manifests. What we say, think, do and believe will have a corresponding effect on others around us because, everything is connected to everything else. We are all one and we are all equal. What we do to others we do to ourselves and vice versa. When we understand this law we also understand that there is no competition and that there is no need to fear not having enough or not being enough.

The Law of Vibrational Frequency - Everything in the universe moves, vibrates and has a frequency including our thoughts, actions, and emotions. What we put out into the environment, through our energy and our vibrations, will come back to us as the same vibrations.

Negative energies attract negative energies and positive energies attract positive energies.

The Law of Action - In order to manifest we must put this law into action to support our thoughts, dreams, words and emotions.

The Law of Correspondence - Light vibrations and motion have their corresponding principles in the universe. "*As above, so below.*" Negative events bring more negative situations and happy events brings more happiness.

The Law of Compensation - The visible effects of our deeds are given to us in blessings and abundance as gifts, money, inheritances, and friendships.

The Law of Potential - The more we tune into our consciousness or soul, the more we will be able to understand our own potential. We are pure consciousness that is responsible for all creations.

The Law of Karma and Reincarnation - Every experience is an opportunity and a blessing to grow and learn from your past as you move forward in time. Our soul has come to earth to learn lessons that are determined from past lives before we came into our current physical body.

The Law of Relativity - Comparing our problems to other people or situational problems we can then put them into proper perspective. No matter how bad we perceive our situation to be, there is always someone or something that is a worse situation.

The Law of Duality - Things that appear as opposites are in fact, only two extremes of the same thing. Examples: Light and dark, hot and cold, two sides of one coin, short and tall, life and death, day and night, near and far, good or bad and so on.

The Law of Rhythm - Everything vibrates and moves to certain rhythms. These rhythms establish cycles, stages of development, and patterns.

The Law of Resistance - Conquering our fears to resolve problems will eliminate our issues. What we resist persists.

The Law of Cause & Effect - This is when an action responds to another reaction. We get back what we put out. *"What goes around comes around."*

The Law of Harmony - It is the purpose of karma and the ultimate balance in life. When we have a conflict, we can then choose harmony, and make the best decisions for the highest potential for our soul.

The Law of Reflection - The traits we find pleasant or unpleasant in others are the traits that exist within us.

The Law of Infinity - Energy cannot be created or destroyed merely by changing its form. There is no time, the past only exists in our mind, as does the future. The only real experience is now. There is an abundance of everything in the universe and there is no such thing as lack, which is a state of mind. If we look for abundance we will find it.

The Law of Gender - All souls are free spirits in the spiritual realm, with no gender discrimination binding them. When humans incarnate they can be attracted to the opposite or same sex gender**.** Masculine and feminine aspects are part of the body of both male and female, in humans, animals, fish, plants, and insects. The physical form does not dictate gender, the soul's energy is really what determines gender. It governs what we know as creation and is required for life to exists in the human, aquatic, bird, animal, insect and some plant life. It does not matter what sexual orientation, race, color of skin, age, or gender a twin flame or soulmates is, their soul, not their bodies meld, together. It is all about energy and vibrational frequency that attracts one to the other to form true love unions.

NOTES

PART II

MANIFESTATION PROCESSES AND COMPONENTS

ASK-BELIEVE-RECEIVE

Chapter 6

Meditation

"Imagination is everything. It is the preview of life's coming attractions."

Albert Einstein

(ASK)

MEDITATION is a technique to focus attention on a particular object, thought, or activity. The reason to use meditation, in the Law of Attraction, is to achieve a mentally clear and emotionally calm, stable, state of mind. It is practiced in many religious traditions such as, Buddhism and Hinduism, to enhance peace and perception of wellbeing, and to reach a higher level of spiritual awareness. It is also used in business and health practices to reduce stress.

There are many modes of meditation but, in this book, you will practice what is called *The Law of Attraction, Visualization Medita*tion. For example, if you want a car, know what make, model, style color and year you desire, and visualize yourself driving it. If you are looking for a new home, visualize the exterior design, the landscaping, the location, the interior furnishings, the decor, and the floorplan, etc. If you want your twin flame or soulmate, visualize every detail such as looks, personality, health, material possessions, home, car, family, and so on. See yourself dancing, walking hand in hand, traveling, kissing, hugging and whatever else you would enjoy doing together.

The Visualization Meditation Technique:

- When you first begin to meditate, find a quiet place in your home or garden.

- If you choose to be outside, relax in the shade of a tree or a covered area.

- There should be no external noise or distractions like a dog barking, a baby crying, a television playing, traffic noise, etc. The sounds you should listen to are the singing of the birds or soft, relaxing, meditation music.

- Sit in a chair that is comfortable or on a floor mat. If you choose a chair, place your feet flat on the ground, and your hands in your lap with palms facing up. If you choose to sit on a floor mat in a yoga position, put your hands on your lap with your palms facing up.

- If you choose to be indoors, sit in a relaxing chair, turn off any bright lights and listen to soft, meditation music or sounds of your choice. Some soothing sounds can be crashing waves with chirping seagulls, rain, rushing waters of a mountain stream or birds singing.

- Focus on the glow of candlelight, a pretty object or favorite picture.

- Close your eyes and breathe in and out slowly until you feel yourself becoming very relaxed.

- As you drift into an altered state of consciousness you will become one with all that is.

- Quiet your thoughts, visualize whatever you desire to manifest, and see it in your mind's eye as though it is happening at that moment.

- Communicate with whomever you want through telepathy as you visualize that person. You can also get answers to your questions as well as send healing and love to someone in need.

- Stay in the meditative state as long as you feel you want to.

- When you are ready to return to an awakened state, take long, slow, deep breaths and gradually open your eyes.

- If possible, try to do this meditation every day to help you relax and move to a higher, vibrational frequency.

You can have as many desires as you want to manifest once you are in a higher, vibrational frequency of 5D. Do not become frustrated when your request has not manifested right away. The universe will send you what you ask for at the perfect time, not the time you want your desires to manifest. If you are not manifesting parking spaces then you are still in 3D and have more work to do. You must believe 100%, that your *divine gifts* will be yours when you are ready to receive them, and your *Inner Guidance System* will give you the directions to location and exact time of manifestation.

Three years had passed before my twin flame manifested and the hardest part was to be patient. He was married and his wife had to leave the relationship before we could meet. I communicated with him through meditation. I closed my eyes, took a few deep breaths, and then he appeared in my mind's eye. He had grey hair and beautiful crystal, blue eyes, exactly like I had envisioned in my *Letter of Intention.* We communicated through telepathy and I asked him, "When will we meet in the physical reality?" he said, "It is not time yet".

The next month I asked the same question during meditation and I received the final answer, "It won't be too much longer." He was right, a few weeks later my *Inner Guidance System* alerted me to go to a singles dance at the local hotel. It was late in the day and I almost ignored the message. But, I got myself dressed, went to the dance and my twin flame manifested that night.

NOTES

Chapter 7

Letter of Intention, Vision Board And The Inner Guidance System

(ASK-BELIEVE)

THE LETTER OF INTENTION is one of the most important *Components* of manifesting your *divine gifts*. It is written in long hand or on the computer to whatever you believe and pray to. You must describe in detail each request, and don't leave anything out or what you ask for won't manifest exactly as you want. Do not use any negative requests like, "I don't want..." always use, "I would like..." If you wnat to attract a love life iwth your twin flame or romantic, soulmate you will find it described in Part III.

My Letter of Intention:

To God: "I would like to live in a self-contained, active, retirement community with golf and tennis facilities. I want a new courtyard villa with a large, fenced in yard. The interior has to have two bedrooms, two bathrooms, light and airy, cathedral ceilings, large kitchen, living room and dining room combination, a screened in lanai,

facing west and a garage. I want to pay under $200,000."
Love, Anne

In 2010 I toured "The Villages", a self-contained, retirement community in central Florida. The realtor showed me four villas, and when I walked into the fourth one, I knew I had found the exact villa I had asked for in my *Letter of Intention*. I bought it for $159,900 and three months later I moved in. Not only did this self- contained community have a multitude of golf courses, it had two, large tennis facilities, dozens of pickleball courts, many adult swimming pools, thousands of interest clubs, as well as music and entertainment every night, and so much more.

(ASK-BELIEVE)

THE VISION BOARD is a large poster board where you will tape pictures and magazine cut outs of the activities you want with your twin flame or romantic soulmate. On the other side of the poster board you tape pictures of everything you desire. If you want a new car go to the dealership and sit in the car, take a test drive, visualize yourself driving it home and into your garage. If you want a new house, go to an open house tour or look online and visualize living in it. If you want a baby or a grandchild, visualize playing with him or her and holding the little one in your arms. Find a picture of the exact pet you desire and see yourself walking, petting, and caring for it. Find pictures of a vacation and see yourself on the beach, cruising, skiing, biking, etc. If you desire a new career visualize yourself doing what you love as the money flows into your bank account. Put these pictures into action, like a movie in your mind, and feel it as though your *divine gifts* have already manifested in your life. Have fun with this process and sooner or later you will have many "WOW" moments, as I have had.

(RECEIVE)

THE INNER GUIDANCE SYSTEM is the most important Law of Attraction Component and without it nothing will manifest. All birds, animals, fish and insects use this *Inner Guidance System* to find food, a mate, build a nest, fly to remote areas and do whatever else it takes to survive. You must be aware that you also have within you, this innate, (GPS) *Inner Guidance System* that directs you to all your *divine gifts.*

Everyone has a conscious mind, a subconscious mind and a spiritual connected mind. It is through your all-knowing, still, small voice that communicates through your spiritual mind. It is not a voice outside of yourself but an inner feeling that tells you something is important that you need to be aware of. Listen carefully and you will be told what time and location you will find what you have asked for. You must be clear headed, free of alcohol and drugs.

Try and stay on a high vibration when making decisions. Don't react when you feel anger, revenge, jealousy, rage, or fear, which can get you into trouble. If it feels right within your gut, and you are sure it is a positive decision, then follow its guidance. When you are getting negative messages not to proceed, it could be a warning that you need to be careful, and/or to be fully aware of the situation you are experiencing.

It is important that you don't get frustrated when you have followed your *Inner Guidance System* directions and nothing has manifested. The Law of Attraction process takes time and practice. The more you use it the better you will become at hearing your messages, and the directions you must follow to manifest what you desire.

After you have learned The Law of Attraction *Principles, Processes* and *Components* you can practice manifesting parking spaces. Before you get to your destination, **ask** for the parking space, *"I want to park in front of the store, restaurant, etc.*", and when you reach the parking area, visualize and **believe** you will get the exact spot you are thinking about. Have patience, drive slowly and listen to your *Inner Guidance System* directing you to the parking space. It might not happen at first but, you should never give up. Once you start to **receive** parking spaces you will have the confidence to manifest so much more when you finally ascend to 5D. Throughout my lifetime, I have always listened to my Inner Guidance System taking me through many twists and turns. If I had not trusted my still, small voice, guiding me through many situations, I don't know where I would be today. I might have stayed in a dull, lonely, comfortable life, even though I knew deep inside, that was not my life's purpose.

I also use my *Inner Guidance System* to help me find an item, like my keys. I ask, "Where are my keys?" I listen carefully and within a few seconds I will get the answer and find my keys. It really works when I am clear headed, alert and aware.

NOTES

Chapter 8

Mood Ascension Scale

"You create your thoughts, your thoughts create your intentions and your intentions create your reality."

Wayne W. Dyer

THE MOOD ASCENSION SCALE is a tool to raise your vibrational frequency and attract more positive people, places and situations into your life. It will show you where your mood level is at any given moment, and give you an understanding of why situations are turning out positive or negative in your life.

In 3D there are two vibrational levels, the lowest level and the mid-level. Throughout the day you might vacillate between feeling happy in 4D and 5D, and the next day drop back to 3D. If you haven't learned the *Processes, Procedures and Components* of the Law of Attraction, you won't be able to stay in 4D and 5D for long. Your goal is to always be in 5D to manifest all your *divine gifts*.

The Mood Ascension Scale ranges from the following levels:

5D – The Highest Vibrational Frequency – Where all positive manifestations takes place and you strive to live every day. Think of positive situations and feel grateful for good health, money in the bank, food on the table, a beautiful home, a pet, a loving family, loving relationships or whatever makes you feel happy, joyful for all you have.

Emotions – Love, joy, happiness, gratitude, positive expectations, empowerment, knowledge, elation, passion, freedom, fearless, devotion, excitement.

4D – The Next Highest Vibrational Frequency – Where pre-manifestation takes place and parking spaces begin to appear. You are now beginning to feel confident that whatever you desire will manifest as long as you stay in 4D and 5D.

Emotions – Eager, hopeful, appreciative, optimistic, enthusiastic, believer, content.

3D – The Neutral Vibrational Frequency – When life throws you a curve ball and you are in a state of flux. It is a place where you would like to make some sort of decisions to get out of feeling uncomfortable. Take one step at a time, reaching for the best feeling thought on the *Mood Ascension Scale.* Continue this process until you start to feel better about your life and/or circumstances.

Emotions – Boredom, pessimism, doubt, frustration, irritation, impatience, annoyed, disappointed, worry, blame, overwhelmed, discouraged.

3D – The Lowest Vibrational Frequency – When you are all the way down in the dumps and you can't seem to shake off your negative mood. You feel awful and are having a hard time getting out of your funk. No one likes to feel these emotions, but sometimes life happens and down you go. It can be due to a loss such as, a death, money, relationship, illness, a job, or other unfortunate situations. Don't despair, this is part of what happens to every human being and is only a detour in your quest for happiness. After you go through the natural process of grieving there will be a time hopefully, sooner than later, when you will be ready to slowly raise your vibrational frequency to a higher level.

Emotions – Sadness, anger, jealousy, hatred, rage, revenge, insecurity, guilt, grief, fear, depression, anxiety, despair, powerless, unworthy

---

Learning the different vibrational levels and moving from one emotional feeling to another takes practice. You cannot jump from sadness to joy or depression to happiness. You must go up the scale step by step, until you start to feel better by changing your negative thoughts to positive thoughts.

Be grateful for what you have in the present and your current situations will soon change. Let go of drama and do the things that make you feel good. Most people live each day between the 3D and 4D emotional levels, with sporadic days in 5D. Your objective is to ascend to 5D and stay there so as to manifest and feel great.

I am not saying that you will not experience the lower, vibrational levels of sadness, grief and disappointment at some point during your life. We all go through trying times and that is normal. You will need time to recoup and you will know when you are ready to move up the scale to feel better.

We all feel the vibrations of someone who is in a bad mood and they can affect everyone around them.

Never allow a person or situation to bring your high vibrational frequency of love, happiness and joy down to the lowest vibrational frequency of anger, rage, fear, intimidation, sadness, hurt, guilt, blame, revenge, etc.

If there is a negative situation surrounding you and you feel verbally attacked, tell that person you will not accept their behavior and if you are in danger, leave immediately. You cannot do your best thinking and problem solving when you are in a state of fear and unhappiness. You know the feeling when your heart rate and blood pressure increases. Try and dissipate the negative situation with love and compassion. If that does not work understand that you cannot control conditions, people, or situations, you can only control your own thoughts and feelings.

Activities To Bring Up Your Vibrations:

- Plant an organic garden, watch the seeds sprout and grow into healthy, nutritious food. Find delicious recipes and savor every bite, knowing it is all your creation.

- If you have children or grandchildren, go to a park and watch them laugh and play on the playground. Afterwards, go to an ice cream store and enjoy a treat together.

- Watch a beautiful sunset.

- Admire the colors of a rainbow after a rain shower.

- Sit in your garden or walk in nature.

- Take a trip to the mountains and go on a hike. Breathe in the fresh smell of the pine trees, listen to the bird sounds and enjoy all that nature has to offer.

- Go to the beach and feel your bare feet in the sand, the warm sun on your skin and the soft wind in your face. Breathe in the salty, fresh air filled with all those good, negative ions. Watch the seagulls flying above the crashing waves and sailboats gliding along the ocean's currents.

- Plant a butterfly garden and enjoy all the species of butterflies gliding in the wind and feeding on their nectar plants. Watch birds flying in the breeze, landing in the trees and chirping to each other.

- Raise butterflies in cages and watch the amazing transformation of an ugly caterpillar transform into a beautiful butterfly in a matter of a few weeks. It is thrilling when you open the cage and the newly hatched butterfly takes flight for the first time!

- Adopt a dog for company and take daily walks in your neighborhood or go to the dog park. You might meet some new dog owner friends. If you don't own a dog, start a dog walking or dog sitting business where you can make some extra money.

- Go to a pond or lake and watch all species of birds, ducks and geese enjoying their freedom, swimming on the water, and taking flight towards another destination. Observe the baby ducklings waddling alongside their mother and father, jumping into the water together and swimming away.

- Dance to your favorite music, alone or with a partner.

- Learn yoga for exercise and health.

- Join interest groups where you will learn something new and meet people of like minds.

- Play or watch a sport that you enjoy.

- Go on a bike ride and enjoy the change in scenery, as you get some exercise.

- Listen to your favorite music and sing along.

- Have a dinner party or cook a delicious meal for someone special.

- Watch a funny movie or your favorite sitcom.

- Find a hobby collecting artifacts or items of interest.

- Remember a great vacation and visualize the next one.

- Enjoy a relaxing massage.

NOTES

PART III

TWIN FLAMES AND SOULMATES

"Life is but a stage and we are merely actors. You share this earth and the experiences with many other souls in the movie that is your life. Begin today to make your life exactly as you desire it to be, with your soulmate or twin flame." (Inspired by Shakespeare)

Anonymous

Chapter 9

Twin Flame History and Mission

"The minute I heard my first love story I started looking for you, not knowing how blind that was. Lovers don't finally meet somewhere, they are in each other all along."

Rumi

Throughout history twin flames have met, joined and served humanity. The spiritual philosophies in the Hindu Verdes, Bhagavad Gita, writers, philosophers, poets and master spiritual teachers of the ancient East and West have written about twin souls.

Plato graphically portrayed the twin soul image 2500 years ago, in the *Symposium Aristophanes*. "*How Zeus struck the soul into two opposite halves, each to wander the earth in search of the other.*" Plato said, "*When one of them meets the other half, the pair is lost in the amazement of love, friendship and intimacy and one will not be out of the other's sight, even for a moment.*"

The Sufis are a mystical, Islamic movement that first appeared in Persia in the eighth century. They said that the eternal principle of the twin flame union is as follows: *"Before incarnation the soul splits into two separate entities. When born into the physical, in separate families, they search for their other half, driven by love."*

Omraam Mikhael Aivanhow was a Bulgarian who wrote in the 1960's Love and Sexuality, part one: *"Every human being possesses a sister soul. When man leaped like a flame, a spark from the bosom of his Creator, he was two in one and each of his two halves was the perfect complement of the other; each of the two halves become separated, each of them taking a different direction and evolving in its own way. During the course of their lives they will meet and, if they recognize each other it is because each carries the image of the other in their soul, a mirror of themselves for which they immediately recognize."*

Edgar Cayce was called the "sleeping profit," in the early 1900's. He spoke about twin souls and states, *"In the beginning the male and female energies were as in one."*

Saint Germain wrote, *"Twin flames are identical resonances of the same frequency within different bodies of energy."*

Marie and Pierre Currie were as close to perfection as could be during their marriage. Their daughter states: *"My mother and father were of equal quality. They formed one of the finest bonds that ever united man and woman. Their two hearts beat together, two bodies united, and two minds who could think together."*

Harriet Taylor and John Mill, were one of the happiest recorded twin flames who met at the end of the 1820's. Together they wrote essays, met daily and exchanged love letters.

Petrarch and Laura were twin flames. Petrarch was the fourteenth century poet laureate of Italy, whose sonnets to Laura are considered the greatest love poems ever written.

Carl Sandburg and Lilian Steichen were twin flames. Carl was a contemporary poet who wrote soul-love letters to his wife, Lilian. He refers to their union as the S and S or two souls of the same intensity, harmony, vibration and equilibrium. They both reorganized a universal religion of humanism and joy in life.

Romeo and Juliet were the most famous twin flame couple ever to be written about by William Shakespeare. Their love story is about two teenagers who fall in love at first sight, marry and risk all for their love.

George Burns and Gracie Allen were a famous radio and television comedy duo who devoted their lives to one another and made the world laugh with their humor. When Gracie died, George visited his wife's grave monthly stating, *"He looked forward to death because on that day he would be with Gracie again, in heaven."*

Queen Victoria and Prince Albert is a love story about English royalty. In 1840, Queen Victoria married her first cousin, Prince Albert and they had nine children. After his death Queen Victoria did not appear in public for three years. She never stopped mourning her husband, wearing black until her death.

The twin flames mission is to take responsibility for themselves and the planet earth, which has lost its way in spiritual consciousness, and is stumbling to exist without it. We are on the brink of a spiritual evolution, a quantum leap in consciousness, that is awakening humanity to its true purpose.

Twin flames are reuniting in great numbers at this time to assist with the 5D ascension process, both at the individual and the planetary level. This 5D frequency will act as a catalyst to help bring about the expected breakthrough as light in the darkness of society's consciousness, within the whole of humanity.

NOTES

Chapter 10

Soulmate and Twin Flame Dynamics

"Maybe we have lived a thousand lives before this one and in each of them we found each other. I know I have spent each life before this one searching for you, for your soul and mine must always come together."

Nicholas Sparks

SOULMATES live in a 3D vibrational frequency. Their relationships can be intense with a lot of lust and excitement, attracted to a specific type of personality and energy. It can be a feeling or a remembrance of a relationship that is locked into your cellular memory from past lives and/or have been preplanned prior to incarnating in your current lifetime.

Romantic soulmate relationships will occur prior to the twin flame meeting. These relationships can help to accelerate growth and learning for each individual soul, to reach higher understandings of unconditional love and unity consciousness. These experiences and personal, spiritual work will prepare the individual to face the intensity of being with their twin flame.

Everyone will have many soulmate relationships throughout their incarnations but, only one twin flame relationship throughout eternity. Some soulmates will choose to have a loving relationship that lasts a lifetime, working through their lessons and learning how to love unconditionally. Other soulmates will be together for a short time, because they still have many lower, 3D lessons and karma to work through.

If soulmates have not learned their 3D lessons they will create an energetic, negative, karmic connection that will be brought into their future soulmate relationships. These lessons are based on conditional, lustful love and sometimes become volatile, purposely hurting their relationship. There is emotional pain and suffering, conflict, struggle, and discord with many up and down days.

This is anything but love because love does not hurt and destroy by abuse, betrayal, lying, cheating, etc. The abusive person must realize what karma they have created in the relationship, and try to make up for their actions. Otherwise, if it is not rectified, this negative, 3D behavior is guaranteed to fail and the relationship will dissolve.

Your vibrational frequency can act as a magnet, repeatedly attracting similar energies and situations. In order to raise your vibration and rid yourself of past, failed, soulmate relationships, you need to release these people from your heart and soul. If you have to see them again, you will need to communicate, without any emotional strings attached, and do the following:

- Formally end the relationship with or without outside therapy, and cut all contact if possible.
- Raise your vibrational frequency by way of the *Mood Ascension Scale,* so you can feel peace, joy and happiness.
- Do not think, dream, or reminisce about your past relationships, they are over.
- Take all the possessions that were given to you and either send them back or get rid of them.
- Take past relationship letters and pictures, and throw them out or burn them outside in a metal bucket.

TWIN FLAMES are an interesting and somewhat, mystical concept of which you might or might not believe or have ever heard of before. Try to keep an open mind and think of it as something new to ponder. It is a fascinating subject and one which makes sense to me, as I have experienced the true meaning of a twin flame as compared to a soulmate relationship. Like most people,

I have had many soulmate relationships of which I have learned important lessons and hopefully, I will try not to repeat them again.

It is said that everyone has a twin flame that comes from one soul. They split into two and plan their next life before incarnating on the earth plane again. They will be conceived into separate families, some sooner and some later, as age differences are common. The twin flames will lead separate, independent lives, learning lessons and overcoming their karma as they experience intense, sometimes rocky, romantic, soulmate relationships.

Before the twin flames reunite, their hearts must be made strong and resilient, experiencing and healing from emotional pain, suffering, grief, and loss.

Sometimes one twin flame is in 5D while the other twin will be vacillating between 3D and 4D. The 5D twin has a responsibility to teach and help the other to transcend the limitation of ego, and to have an understanding of unconditional love and oneness. If this feat is not accomplished in their present lifetime, and one twin flame is still stuck in their 3D negative state, they will have to reincarnate together again in another lifetime. Hopefully, this will be their final time in an earthly incarnation before ascending together in 5D, and returning to the God Source for eternity.

Whether you meet your twin flame in the early or later years, you will connect like a magnet and it will be an instant recognition. Everything has been set up and preplanned so as to recognize each other. After your first conversation, a familiar word, place or circumstance is spoken about and a surge of energy goes through your bodies. Emotions, feelings and awareness are like no other and there is a heightened, inner awakening. You might find out that you both have worked in similar jobs or have the same family background.

For a twin flame union to thrive and advance spiritually they must agree to admire, appreciate, be kind, affectionate, have empathy, have sympathy, good rapport, understanding, patience, tolerance, and keep a sense of humor under stressful situations. Twin flames are forever connected and the pain is deeply felt when they are apart or have disagreements.

Like any human relationship, it isn't easy at their first meeting. There is a pull and tug for a while until both come to a place of peace, bliss and unconditional love. Twin flames may have differences in ages, same or different sexual orientation, geographic locations, morals, beliefs, races or income brackets, to name a few.

When twin flames are together and one dies prematurely, the remanding twin flame might remarry for love and/or companionship. The twin flame who is left on the earth plane will always be in the heart and soul of their twin flame who has unfortunately died prematurely. When they are go back to the heavenly realm, they plan their next incarnation with their twin flame, and continue their spiritual journey together.

If you feel you are ready to manifest your twin flame you must first write a *Letter of Intention* and create a *Vision Board.*

A TWIN FLAME LETTER OF INTENTION is written in long hand or on the computer to create a detailed, physical description of your twin flame so that you will immediately recognize him/her when you meet. It is like designing a picture within your mind, describing their outer appearance and desired traits. Write all the positive attributes you want and whatever is important to you. You must be specific, and do not leave anything out, or what you desire won't manifest exactly as you had asked. You can always change anything at any time. If a negative trait surfaces, that you did not expect to be present in your twin flame relationship, it is probably karma that you both have to work through. Before you meet you will connect through dreams, meditations, visualization, and the activities you want to do together, as through your twin flame has already manifested.

- **Body Type:** Statue, body build, weight, height, age, hair style and color, eye color, good health, etc.

- **Traits:** Kind, intelligent, responsible, sensual, outgoing, sense of humor, happy, empathetic, respectful, committed, generous, confident, educated, quiet, reliable, positive, self-assured, patient, sensitive, etc.

- **Likes:** Dancing, movies, shows, cruising, travel, golf, tennis, scuba, biking, skiing, gardening, cooking, painting, writing, crafts, reading, sports, lake or beach activities, mountain hiking, dogs and other animals, style of car, style of home, etc.

- **Beliefs:** Religious, spiritual, political, investing, world affairs, financial markets, etc.

- **Family:** Loves children, has a close knit and loving family who celebrate holidays together, etc.

- **Social:** Socializes with friends, relatives and neighbors, putters around the house, clubs, hobbies, charities, parties, volunteering, etc.

- **Sexuality:** Strong libido, sexy, sensual, patient, passionate, cuddles, holds your hand, romantic, physical touching, massages, etc.

The universal energies will match up your requests and align your vibrations to your twin flame but, only when you have ascended to the 5D vibrational frequency. Otherwise, you have more work to do on yourself and will continue to meet many more romantic soulmates.

A TWIN FLAME VISION BOARD is designed to tape pictures of activities you want to do with your twin flame. You can add or remove anything at any time. Concentrate on the pictures as though you already have your twin flame in your life.

Twin fame communication is telepathic and is more common and natural within twin flame relationships than within soulmate relationships. This type of communication occurs frequently, and each twin flame can pick up on the other's thoughts and feelings from great distances. They find themselves calling, emailing and texting one another at the exact time when they are tuned into one another's vibrational frequency.

Verbal telepathy is a communication without speaking, via a spiritual connection, and having these words heard between each other. Sensory telepathy can be from taste, smell, sound or sight. Emotional telepathy is when happy thoughts are sent, are both connected, and have more empathy and emotional support for each other.

The twin flame who is more spiritually evolved will have a stronger telepathic ability to transmit than the other.

When emotional and physical impediments are removed between the twin flames, the connection becomes stronger and their vibrations are lifted to higher frequencies that quickens the telepathic connections between them.

In the 3D vibrational frequency, most soulmates are relying solely on spoken language. In the 5D frequency, twin flames not only communicate through telepathy but they communicate by way of their heart chakra. This type of communications can be very strong and intense, opening to enormous feelings of unconditional love. It is very important to keep your hearts and thoughts pure and positive because, it has an immediate effect on your twin flame who can experience the same thoughts, emotions and feelings.

My twin flame and I communicate telepathically, when I think about something and he says the same thing, at the same time. This has happened quite often throughout our eight years together. The first time it happened was when I asked, "What kinds of perfumes would you like me to wear?" Before he answered, I heard within my mind, the exact brands of the two perfumes I was thinking of.

My Letter of Intention example:

God, please send me my twin flame as soon as possible. He must be healthy, height 5'10, weight 170, blue eyes, a lot of grey hair, between 65-70 years old, caring, committed, understanding, thoughtful, dedicated, patient, romantic, dependable, good morals, happy personality with a sense of humor, intelligent, passionate lover, confident, kind, respectful, adventurous, honest, college educated, lives close by in a beautiful home, upscale car, loves to travel, likes the same food, same lifestyle and interests, has a close knit family and many friends, spends his summers at his lake house. Thank you, Love Anne

He manifested exactly as I had written in my Letter of Intention.

NOTES

Chapter 11

Soulmate and Twin Flame Love And Sexuality

"Psychological penetration is love, which is far deeper, far more significant, far more beautiful, far more human then sexual penetration which is a very superficial thing. The third kind of penetration is when two consciousnesses meet, merge and melt into each other."

Osho

ROMANTIC SOULMATES who are in the 3D frequency, have sexual interaction for stimulation only. These types of sexual relationships, that are just based on the physical satisfaction, are ego driven to satisfy sexual needs rather than the spiritual giving, and unconditional love of the twin flames. Their lack of love often demands continual compromise to make the partnership work.

There also exists a close, romantic, soulmate relationship when there is respect, love and a great sexual experience. This is when romantic soulmates claim to "be in love" but, they still need to work on their 3D issues and persevere. They will stay in their relationship for many personal reasons such as children, family, financial, etc., until death do they part.

TWIN FLAMES have very different interactions between the couple, as compared to romantic soulmates. The twin flame relationship cannot be romanticized or idealized and is not about lustful desire or dependency. They have an authentic and divine love that goes beyond the 3D ego. When twin flames have reached the ultimate state of 5D, they accept and love each other unconditionally, and are secure and trusting, knowing their love is spiritual in nature. They are true love souls and when they live their truth from within, love just flows naturally from the other.

You must be love and be your true self to give love and share it back to your twin flame. With twin flames, sex ceases to be just an act because they come together as two halves, merging together as one. It is not just body satisfying but a soul gratifying feeling of physical and spiritual wellbeing. Sex is a state of the body and love is a state of the mind. They love to feel closeness when cuddling skin to skin as their high, vibrational energy melds together.

NOTES

Chapter 12

Soulmate and Twin Flame Relationship Differences

SOULMATES can be lifetime lovers, friends, neighbors, family and have wonderful, loving, and supportive relationships. But, there may also be many difficult soulmate relationships, as specified in the following list:

Soulmate Relationships:

- Lack of trust and deep intimacy.
- Blame and past hurts are projected onto each other.
- The relationship feels difficult even though it was easy at the beginning.
- Envy or jealousy when one or the other achieves success.
- Co-dependency for a sense of happiness and neediness.

- Sex is wanted more by one person than the other.
- Not willing to commit to a long-term relationship.
- Does not want to work on their relationship issues.
- High level of stress or annoyances.
- Wanting the other to change their looks, behavior and their way of life.
- Controlling and/or dominating the other.
- Putting pride, ego, and the importance of monetary and material gain before the importance of the relationship.
- Keeping score, how much one does for the other.
- Not being aware or taking responsibility for hurtful thoughts, words and feelings
- Lack of support of each other.
- Yelling, swearing, throwing things and other out of control behavior.

When presently experiencing one or more of these soulmate relationship situations, do not leave before trying to work it out. If you have reached a stalemate or cannot resolve your problem(s) on your own, seek professional help to either resolve the situation or move on. It is important that you learn from these relationship lessons so you do not repeat them again and again, becoming stuck in a vicious cycle.

TWIN FLAMES are the ultimate relationship most people strive for. When you meet this person, you will definitely know it is your twin flame as compared to your soulmate, and even though there will be some lessons to learn they are different from soulmate lessons.

Twin Flame Relationships:

- There is an overwhelming sense of love, affection and attraction.

- There is a sense of completion and you feel whole once you meet.

- You find that your athletic abilities, skills, and knowledge complement one another.

- You have unconditional love for each other.

- Through your *Inner Guidance System*, you had a feeling to be in a certain place at a certain time, finding your twin flame waiting there for you.

- You never criticize or belittle one another.
- You have created a *Letter of Inten*tion with the attributes and traits of your twin flame for identification, and when you meet they fit the exact description of what you have asked for.
- A new beginning happens in your life. You find that you both are enjoying the journey together.
- You might have mutual friends, family or someone you know that has had a friendship with your twin flame before you met.
- You have the ability to feel each other's emotions, whether they are happy or sad, even from a distance.
- Before and after meeting there is an ability to contact one another through meditation.
- No matter what the obstacles are there is an intense desire to be together.
- When you are not together you are always in touch by e-mail, text or phone.
- Time flies when you are together.

- You both have telepathic communication and you are surprised when the subject matter you are thinking about is then express by your twin flame, at that exact moment.

- You are comforted by their presence, never feeling possessed.

- You may find that you are mirror images and sometimes resemble each other with the same profile, shape nose, expressions and smile.

- You have similar interests, like the same foods, activities, hobbies and vacations among other things.

- You feel similar body aches and pains and know when the other is ill or hurting.

- You do not build walls or barriers.

- You do not lose your identities when you both become more as one.

- There are no barriers when you have obstacles to overcome together.

- The relationship is totally open, as it evolves naturally and often rapidly.

- You almost always meet through unusual circumstances or situations that were totally unexpected and unplanned.

- Looking for your twin flame usually does not bring the two of you together.

- You know that you will be together for eternity and for some deeper purpose.

- You feel more alive since your reunion.

- There is a very sacred sense of intimacy and a feeling of divine inspired wholeness that one finds within a twin soul relationship.

- You never think of receiving in return when you bring joy, relief or nurturing to your twin flame.

- You may still have karma with your twin flame from previous lives but, the two of you resolve it with total forgiveness and unconditional love.

- You don't hide your secrets. You are truthful and respective of one another.

- Neither of you are dependent on the other for your sense of self and you know who you are, with or without your twin flame.

- Sex is a sacred act that celebrates your unconditional love.
- You will never intentionally use anger or hurt towards one another. You trust, have patience and accept their weaknesses.
- There is freedom within the relationship without the need for control or ownership and there are no restrictions.
- Your twin flame will inspire your creativity.
- You do not pretend to be someone other than who you are nor do you compete with one another.
- There is a lot of synchronicity.
- You are truly meant for one another.
- You love each other for uniqueness and individuality.
- You recognize there is a deeper spirituality that manifests and find that you have become reconnected to your higher self.
- You both will serve humanity to gain knowledge of your soul's purpose.

- You are one with everything in the universe.

The Twin Flame Stages:

Preparing -- Before meeting your twin flame, you will experience many 3D karmic, soulmate relationships. These relationships allow you to awaken, grow spiritually, learn self-love, and work on the issues you had with previous relationships. You will discard all past baggage and always love yourself before loving someone else.

Anticipating – When you have ascended to 5D your first meeting with your twin flame will happen when you least expect it. When you meet you will feel a magnetic pull towards this person. Your souls will have already recognized each other in the present lifetime.

Developing – There is a connection through the unusual synchronicity between your souls. As you continue your interactions you will feel the connection deepening and the unconditional love for your twin flame will continue to grow.

Separation – You split up for a while when all your emotions and feelings are intensified and you or your twin flame are not ready for this intense relationship. Not doing the past inner work in the first stage may allow the negative emotions to take control. This is the "runner and chaser stage". The runner assumes they are losing control and is the one who is less mature and not prepared for the intense relationship.

Reunion - You both have managed to let go of emotional baggage and there is only unconditional love, harmony and a feeling of bliss. This takes place when the twin flames become one again and both have realized how important and bonded the relationship is. Other people are aware of this high vibrational energy when around twin flames.

NOTES

Chapter 13

Manifesting Your Twin Flame or Not

"Our universe grants every soul a twin – a reflection of themselves – the kindred spirit – and no matter where they are or how far away they are from each other – even if they are in different dimensions, they will find one another – this is destiny; this is love."

Julie Dillo

If many years have passed and your twin flame has not manifested in the physical, then you probably are not spiritually ready to come together in the present lifetime. No matter how much you plead, cry, pray and beg for your twin flame to manifest, it is not happening, even if you think you are ready and have tried to do everything the Law of Attraction says to do. So, what could it be? You still might have past or present issues and baggage to release or your vibrations are not high enough. Maybe you did not plan to meet in this present lifetime or one is still in the higher realm and decided not to reincarnate. There are so many reasons beyond our reality.

Some twin flames do not incarnate in the physical together every lifetime but, remain on the other side to provide help and spiritual guidance that is very important to spiritual growth. If you are not with your twin flame it could be that you both made a plan before incarnation that you would be connected in the spiritual realm instead of the physical realm.

You will continue to have soulmate relationships in the physical, to enable you to work through your 3D issues and karma. If it is meant for your twin flame to manifest it will happen at the perfect time, place, and when you least expect it.

If you are feeling frustrated and disappointed that your twin flame isn't manifesting, these negative vibrational frequencies could also be holding you back from meeting in the physical. You might have to wait longer than you want because it is not the right time. Your twin flame could be living far away and will need to relocate to be closer to one another.

When in the process of a divorce they are not ready to be with you or it is not feasible to end their relationship at this time, especially when there are children involved. Do not try to intervene or persuade someone to leave a committed relationship, it must be their choice to do so. Soulmate relationships must first be dismantled in a natural way by their lessons learned or not learned. Current karma contracts must be lived fully with honor, honesty and love. Only, if there is unhappiness in their current, committed relationship, it might then be an easy decision to leave.

If you are in a romantic, soulmate relationship or marriage and are thinking of ending the relationship because you think you have found your twin flame, this can be a serious decision and will take a lot of soul searching and possibly therapy.

It is a battle of the heart and mind when contemplating leaving your current relationship to be together with your twin flame. Maybe, at some future time, the dynamics will change and you will be reunited if it is meant to be in this lifetime. There are so many stories of twin flames in other committed relationships who become single again and the universe brings them together.

NOTES

Chapter 14

When a Twin Flame Leaves

"I have come to realize that it matters not where I am on earth, or in spirit, or among the stars, the pain of losing a twin flame never fades."

Michelle Gordon

When your twin flame dies and you feel that part of you is gone, you go through great pain and sorrow, and cannot seem to find peace for what seem like a long time of grieving. You search to find a way to understand why this happened when you have been with the love of your life. But know, your twin flame will be with you again, either in spirit in the afterlife or in another lifetime, and this might bring you peace to your broken heart.

One never knows the answers to why a love one dies prematurely. Yes, there is a deep sense of loss and it is exceptionally painful. But, despite the pain and sorrow of life, it is always important to understand and remember that everything does happen according to plan.

Each soul has a time to be born and a time to die and this is part of our life process. Be grateful that you had the special time on earth and that you can connect and receive messages of love and comfort from your deceased twin flame in your dreams as well as during meditation.

As time goes by you must move on and interact with other people. You should never stop your life and fall into depression or despair as that just brings you into a negative vibration where you won't manifest anything positive. It is possible that in the near future you might even meet a romantic soulmate that you can have a loving relationship with. Use The Law of Attraction and your *Mood Ascension Scale* to get on with your life and be happy.

The Chaser and The Runner phase happens in about twenty percent of twin flame relationships. In this relationship, one twin flame has not grown spiritually or learned unconditional love. The other twin flame is more spiritual and has already ascended to 5D. This type of relationship can turn volatile and if not rectified, they will go their separate ways and break up because of fear of the intensity of their union. The runner leaves and the chaser tries hard to get the relationship back but, only when the runner is ready to return and work on their special union will they reunite. The chaser is usually more spiritually advanced and understands how The Law of Attraction works, whereas the runner has trouble understanding this concept of spirituality and how it applies in their relationship.

Chaser:

- Makes the mistake of being too needy and/or opening up too much early on in the relationship and scares their twin flame away.

- Has to be patient and not critical, demanding, or clingy towards the runner or they will run even faster.

- Feels the emotions of the runner as a deep loss. The chaser will have more emotional pain if they have had past abandonment issues but, must realize it is not personal.

- Give them space to work on their issues and don't interfere. They will return on their own time when and if they are ready.

- Keep busy with activities and surround yourself with positive people and environments.

- Do not dwell on the loss as this will bring down your vibrational frequency, and is not good for The Law of Attraction to work in a positive way.

Runner:

- Is afraid of their feelings from past emotions that have not been dealt with in the present.

- Becomes overwhelmed and flees the twin flame relationship.

- Worries about change, failure, loss, or surrendering to unconditional love when they are not ready to deal with these emotions.

- Looks for "safe relationships" and will shy away from commitment, distancing themselves from their twin flame.

- Has a strong feeling of emptiness when both hearts are broken.

- Still has a strong attraction and an array of emotions but will not be able to manage and control these feelings.

- Has never felt such emotional pain and despair in any other current life relationship.

- Is not prepared for the mental, emotional and spiritual aspects of this connection and will project back to the other twin flame all the things they do not like, do not understand, deny, reject and refuse to accept into their life.

- Will not communicate, have hot and cold behaviors and deny there is a twin flame connection.

In order for the runner and the chaser to heal and know that the relationship is worth salvaging they first have to reconnect with themselves before they can reconnect with each other. They need to give each other space and at some future time, if it is meant to be in this present lifetime, they might come to terms when they can understand their feelings and emotions. The key to a twin flame soul connection is in accepting one another entirely and continue to love each other unconditionally, regardless of all the imperfections that their twin flame presents.

The twin flames are aware of their soul consciousness no matter how much they fight it. When they both are ready to work on themselves in a positive way, and accept that the relationship is worth salvaging, they will reunite again to focus on their spiritual journey and be in harmony. The key to a twin flame soul connection is in accepting one another entirely and loving themselves and others, without conditions, expectations or attachments in an unconditional, divine love.

NOTES

PART IV

THE FIFTH DIMENSION

"Everything your heart desires will manifest in the 5th dimensional vibrational frequency."

Anne Lauren

The Meaning of the Numbers 11:11

When you start seeing **11:11** on clocks, birthdays, dates, license plates, etc., it means that you have reached a higher, vibrational frequency of awakening and ascension, and your wishes or *divine gifts* will soon manifest. It is the universe's way of urging you to pay attention to your heart, your soul and your inner intuition. The opportunities and synchronicities around you should not be ignored. You are waking up from the illusion world of 3D that everyone is plugged into, and coming into your true power, new adventures, and new paths in 5D. There are no accidents or coincidences, everything is happening in divine order and you are becoming more aware that you are one with all that is.

When you see the **11:11** sequence of numbers it also means your twin flame is ready to manifest. The numbers represent the mirrored souls of the twin flames. If in the spiritual realm, they will appear to you in meditation and dreams and you will begin to communicate with each other. If you are to meet in the physical, your *Inner Guidance System* will give you directions as to when, where, and how you will meet. If you have already met, the numbers will verify that this is your true, twin flame.

The universe tries to show you the way through small signs but, in order to recognize these signs, you must be open and spiritually ready to receive them. In numerology the number **11:11** sequence is a master number used to communicate with your spiritual guides and guardian angels to manifest your wishes.

Flying High In The Sky

FLIGHT 11:11 INSTRUCTIONS

By Anne Lauren

Good morning and welcome to Flight 11-11.

There will be no baggage on this plane.

Fasten your seatbelts and be ready for takeoff to the 5th dimension.

Make sure your positive attitude and gratitude are secured and locked in the upright position.

All your self-destruct devices: pity, selfishness, anger, hurts, resentments discouragements and negativity should be put away and turned off at this time.

Should you lose your positive attitude during flight, press the red button above your seat to raise your vibrational frequency before helping other passengers who are on the lower, 3rd dimensional frequency.

When we have reached the altitude of the 5th dimensional frequency, there will be an abundance of love, joy and happiness for all.

God, your pilot is ready for takeoff. Have a blessed journey.

Angel Appearances

We all have guardian angels who appear to us whenever we are in need. Most people, who are still in the 3D reality are not aware of these manifestations, and will just assume they are just nice people who are around to help. But, when you have ascended to the 5D reality your guardian angels will appear in human form and ask, *"Can I help you?"* They will give you a message or help you with a problem, and when you are not looking, they disappear into thin air. Because I have had so many angels help me, I will never doubt that they exist. The following are my stories I hope you will enjoy reading:

Lost Dog – One evening my two beagles had escaped and time was of the essence to find them before it grew dark. The male beagle returned home but, the female was nowhere in sight. She was not the smartest dog and did not know the neighborhood. She had never run away before and it was too late to drive all over town looking for her. All I could do was pray and visualized she would soon come back home.

The next day I received a phone call from the local police. They found my telephone number on my dog's tag and informed me that, "A lady **(an angel)**, was driving in town and saw a dog walking along the road. She had a strong feeling to stop her car, rescue the dog and bring it into the police department." My prayer for help was answered and my beagle was finally back home, safe and sound.

Lost Wallet – I was in the market getting some food off a shelf when I heard the magnet on my purse snap closed. As I looked around I saw two women running down the aisle and I checked my purse and found my wallet was missing. I reported the incident to the manager but, he didn't have any desire to chase the thieves. Without my wallet I had no license, credit cards or money, and I prayed and visualized that everything would be returned as soon as possible.

The next day, I got a phone call from a convenience store manager, who informed me that, "A man, **(an angel)** with long hair and a beard, found my wallet as he was walking along a busy highway. He brought it into the store and then he left". I rushed over to the store to retrieve my wallet. I saw that my credit cards and license were there but, my money was gone. I learned a lesson to never leave my purse in my shopping cart while getting food off a shelf.

Puppy – For many years I had visualized and asked, in my *Letter of Intention*, for a long hair, miniature, female dachshund, less than a year old. While reading the ads in the newspaper I came across one that said, "Female, miniature dachshund rescue, needing a loving home." I had a strong desire to go see her and when I arrived at the pet store she was not the dog that I had visualized and prayed for. I was about to leave when I spotted a small, sweet, docile female beagle in a cage and decided to walk her around the outside of the pet store so I could make a decision to adopt her or not.

An hour went by and I grew tired so, I found a chair next to the entrance of the pet store and sat down with the beagle. Within a few minutes a lady, **(an angel),** walked by holding a dachshund puppy in her arms. I asked her, "Where did you get your puppy*?"* She told me where and said that she had bought three more that she wanted to sell. One was a female, miniature dachshund, long hair, seven months old. I had been looking for the exact dog and was anxious to see her. Later that day she brought the puppy to my house She was exactly as I had visualized for the past five years. I bought her for $250, a real steal for such a beauty.

My little dachshund, now ten years old, is so sweet, and loving. She has given me so much joy and happiness. If I had not listened to my *Inner Guidance System,* telling me to go to the pet store that morning, spending time walking around the pet store with the beagle, sitting down on the chair by the front door and speaking to the lady with the dachshund puppy, I would never have gotten my precious fur baby. The Law of Attraction is all about timing and the most important component is *The Inner Guidance System* or inner voice that says, "Go now, it is time!*"*

Lost Luggage: – I was traveling through Orlando International Airport and I checked my many items through security. I rode the tram to the plane hub and when I got off, I realized I left my carryon bag in security. I got back on the tram and found it eerie when I realized that it was the middle of the day and I was the only passenger. Holding onto the pole, I felt a tap on my shoulder. I turned around and saw a man, **(an angel),** standing in back of me with an Orlando personnel tag around his neck. He asked, "Can I help you?" "Yes", I replied. "I left my bag in security and have no idea which line I was in." He said, "Not to worry, I will take you to your bag." We got off the tram and walked to one of the many security checkouts. He pointed to a bag and sure enough, it was mine. I was so excited to get my bag back and when I turned to thank him he had disappeared.

Delayed Plane – My plane had been delayed for a few hours due to a storm. No one had been given any information when the plane was to arrive, and after a few hours of waiting, everyone became upset and annoyed. I told them, "I will find the pilot and get some information on the flight status." They looked at me with blank faces, I am sure they were thinking, how could I get the information when they tried and failed?

I got up from my seat and walked down the gateway. Suddenly, I spotted a pilot walking towards me while looking at his phone. I asked him, "Are you the pilot flying to Stewart Airport in New York?" "Yes," he replied. I asked, "Do you have any idea when it will arrive?" He pointed to the flight information on his phone and said, "The plane was delayed due to a thunderstorm and is now on the runway waiting for clearance, it should arrive within the hour." I thanked him and walked back to my seat. I informed everyone that I had just talked to the pilot and he said our plane would be here within the hour.

The passengers seemed perplexed that I actually found our pilot and got all the flight information. An hour later the plane finally arrived and the distraught passengers began boarding. A Mariachi band and singer manifested next to our gate and began to play as the passengers clapped and danced to the uplifting music. Everyone was in a happy mood as they boarded the plane. What were the chances that the pilot, **(an angel),** manifested at the perfect time and place to give me the flight information I needed? How did a band appear out of nowhere, raising everyone's vibrations? That was the first time I had ever seen a band play at a boarding gate. It all felt surreal.

Lost Computer – I was flying back from Stewart Airport to Orlando and checked my bags through security. I had my dog with me, her stroller, my backpack and computer. I gathered up my things and proceeded to walk to my gate. I was in line to board the plane when I felt a tap on my shoulder and turned around to see a blond lady, **(an angel)**, standing in back of me. She said, "You left your computer in security." I bent down to look through my backpack and sure enough, my computer was missing. I got up and turned to thank her but she disappeared.

I rushed back to security and retrieved my computer, then hurried back to the gate as the plane's door was closing. I was so thankful **(an angel)** appeared to give me the message otherwise, all my hard work on this book would have been lost along with all my other important information.

Car Repair – I love butterflies and belong to the Butterfly Club of The Villages. They have a beautiful, butterfly garden at a nearby church and so I decided to go see it. I drove into the church parking lot and as I pulled into a parking spot I heard my front bumper bang into a concrete barrier. I got out to find a part from my car had fallen off, and was laying on the ground. Suddenly, I heard a voice say "Can I help you?" I looked up and saw a young man standing by my car. "Yes," I said, "A part fell off my car and I can't put it back on." He replied, "I will see what I can do." He knelt down, looked under the car, and placed the broken part back where it belonged. He then informed me, "You should be good to go." I thanked him and said, "You must be **(an angel)**?" He smiled and replied, "Yes, this is the church parking lot." When I got up off the ground I looked around and he had disappeared, nowhere to be found.

Market - I was in the market looking for some canned claims when I saw them on the top shelf. I could not reach them and was thinking about how I was going to get the cans down when I saw a very tall man walking down the aisle towards me. I asked him if he would get me a few cans down from the top shelf? "No problem." he said. I thanked him and said, "You are **(an angel).**" He walked away with a big smile on his face, and I was delighted to get the clams for my linguine dinner.

My Manifestations

Throughout my life I have had the ability to get whatever I wanted just by thinking, wishing and praying for it. It was just a belief system that seemed to work for me and at the time, I didn't even know about The Law of Attraction. The following are my many manifestation stories from an early age up to the present. I hope they will inspire you to believe you can do the same:

First Dog – On my fifth birthday, I wished for and visualized a little puppy of my own. My aunt called mom and told her that she had a surprise for me and to come to her house as soon as possible. When I walked into her kitchen I saw a brown box and ran over to see what was inside. To my surprise, it was a little eight-week-old, dachshund puppy. I fell in love when I picked him up and held him in my arms. My birthday wish had manifested and that was the start of my belief that wishes do come true.

High School Club – In my junior year of high school the girls in my grade were forming social clubs. There was a club for the most popular girls, another for the smart, geeky girls and another for the not so popular girls. I had been friendly with many of the most popular girls since junior high school. I really wanted to be in the club and visualized having fun with my friends and going to the parties with the popular boys. A few days later I got the call that they had voted me in. I was ecstatic, my high school social life manifested just the way I had wanted.

Career – I was accepted at UCLA, my college of choice, and studied to become an obstetric nurse. I trained in a hospital and had my own newborn care business. Even though I loved the adorable newborns and enjoyed teaching new parents how to care for their baby, I realized that it was not a good career for a single girl and I switched careers.

I interviewed for a sales assistant position in a stock brokerage business and was hired. To advance my position, I studied "The New York Institute of Finance, Stock Exchange Course." I passed the test and worked in the corporate and municipal bond research department. Later in life, I passed the Real Estate Sales Course and worked in a real estate office. I bought, sold and rented out condominiums and villas. It all manifested exactly as I had planned and my investment careers were a lot more lucrative than being a nurse.

Soulmate – In my early twenties I met a good looking, hunky guy at my friend's pool. We were attracted to each other right away and we dated for three years. He loved to ski and moved to a ski resort in northern California called Mammoth Lakes. To be near him, I took up the sport. I visualized having the time of my life with my boyfriend, living in Mammoth in a new condo with a big, stone fireplace overlooking snowcapped mountains.

It wasn't long before he wrote me a letter inviting me to join him. I quit my job, drove up to the ski resort and bought the new condominium I had visualized. We spent a wonderful winter and summer together skiing, hiking, backpacking, camping and fishing in the beautiful Sierra Nevada Mountains. At the end of the summer we got married in Los Angeles and drove to New Jersey where his family lived.

As a teenager, I had visualized what my life would be like married to the man I loved, with two kids, a boy first and then a girl, living in a 5,000 square foot contemporary ranch home. It all manifested exactly as I had visualized.

Miraculous Healing – I had lifted very heavy boxes of ceramic tiles from my car into the house. I soon developed a very bad pain in my lower back that radiated down my right thigh. I thought I pulled a muscle and for weeks the pain never went away.

I am a holistic person and I don't take medicine or see a doctor unless I absolutely have to. I heard that quartz crystals transmit energy, are used in watches and radios, and can possible help transmit healing prayers. So, I purchased a beautiful crystal, a healing book and practiced what I read while concentrating on getting rid of my back pain. The next day I let the dog out the back door and slipped on the icy steps. The pain radiated down my leg and was so bad I had to crawl back into the house and call my husband. He knew it sounded bad and called an ambulance to take me to the hospital.

In the emergency room, I was told, "I had a large, ruptured disk in my back and I had to be admitted to the hospital, with the possibility of having surgery." So much for self-healing! I called my best friend to tell her what had happened. She notified our prayer group and told me that they were going to send me a healing at 7:00 pm. That evening I sat up in bed with my crystal in my hand and visualized my back healed.

The next morning the doctors came in and examined me. When they realized I could move my leg without pain, they looked at each other and said, "It must be her endorphins working!" I had an MRI that showed the disc had shrunk back into the spinal column overnight and I was pain free from that day on. I believe when a miraculous healing takes place, through prayer and visualization, it is truly a divine intervention.

Florida – As I sat by the woodstove in my New Jersey home watching the snow fall, I visualized myself on a sandy beach, soaking up the warm Florida sunshine. My husband refused to visit Florida or buy a winter getaway, and after 17 years of a rocky marriage, we got divorced.

I had visited my best friend in Boca Raton, Florida many times and knew that was the place I wanted to live. I was happy to say goodbye to my old life and the New Jersey winters. I packed up my belongings, hired a mover and off I went to Florida with my teenage daughter. My son stayed with his father and soon went off to college.

I bought a new townhouse on a lake, where I loved watching the beautiful sunsets from my lanai. I spent twenty happy years enjoying the beach, playing tennis, golf, Mahjongg and Canasta with wonderful friends I had met throughout the years. Even though moving to Florida and starting a whole new life took a lot of soul searching and energy, it all manifested just as I had asked for and visualized.

Money – My sister was dying of cancer and I had sent her a big bouquet of flowers and balloons to her hospital room. The next day, while I was shopping, I got a call from my bother-in-law that she had passed away. My *Inner Guidance System* gave me a message that I should walk down a certain aisle in the store and I followed the directions. I looked down and noticed five, twenty-dollar bills on the floor, the exact amount I had spent on my sister's flowers. It was strange that no one else had noticed the money. I picked up the bills and examined them. To my surprise, it was real money and not a joke.

That night my phone rang around 2 am and woke me up. I answered it and no one was there. I felt that my sister was giving me a sign that she was still around in spirit form, thanking me for sending her flowers.

Retirement – I was nearing retirement age and decided it was time to move to a "self-contained city", with many activities and amenities. I met some new friends who spoke about a great community called "The Villages", one hour north of Orlando, and gave me some information about the retirement community. I spent a few months on the internet researching the area before I drove up to see this amazing place.

I spent a few days looking at real estate and made the decision to buy a brand new, bright and sunny villa with a lanai overlooking a large, fenced-in-yard for my dog. It was the exact home and price I had visualized.

I rented my townhouse in Boca for two years and moved into my new villa. I joined single groups, played golf, tennis, Pickleball, Mahjongg, Canasta, and founded The Dachshund Club, for which there are now over 80 members. I always wanted to start a club and this one has become very successful. We meet once a month for "Wiener Walks" and the adorable dachshunds get dressed up for each holiday celebration. Everything manifested at the perfect time and place.

Twin Flame – Since my divorce, I dated hundreds of men, had many relationships, and except for a few, most were a big disappointment. Why did I have to date so many men I had nothing in common with nor was physically attracted to? Answer: It was to learn more lessons about myself. To raise my 3D, vibrational frequency from being lonely, unhappy, needy, and desperate, to a more positive 5D vibrational frequency of self-love, as well as to know what I wanted and did not want in a relationship.

When I moved to The Villages I realized that it is a great place for married or cohabiting couples but, not so great if you are a single woman. Most of the single men I was meeting seem to enjoy playing the field because they had a big field to "play in", and the ratio was eight women to every man!

I joined a singles club and was very fortunate to have met a very nice man who changed my life. He had a twin flame and they were very much in love. We became friends and I told him about my dilemma. He said, "Before you can manifest your twin flame you need to bring up your vibrations. You are thinking in a negative way and I hear you say that you are not meeting anyone that meets your expectations. The Law of Attraction will manifest whatever a person is thinking about, and that is why you are manifesting relationships you do not want." He invited me to join his Law of Attraction group so I could meet people of like minds and make some new friends.

I studied The Law of Attraction*: Principles, Processes and Components* and put it all into action. Most importantly, I had to be patient with a strong desire to accomplish this feat. Even though I was in my late 60's, and started to get anxious, I never gave up.

Every month my church had a meditation and I visualized a handsome man with beautiful blue eyes and a head of grey hair. We communicated telepathically, and I asked him, “When are we going to meet in the physical?” He answered, “It is not time yet.” A month later, I asked again in meditation, “So, is it time?” He answered, “Pretty soon.”

It wasn’t long before I got a loud and clear message from my *Inner Guidance System*. It said, “You must go tonight to a single’s dance at The Waterfront Hotel.” At first, I tried to ignore the message because, I do not enjoy single events and was not in the mood to go alone. Unwillingly, I got dressed, and called my friend who met me at the dance.

I was talking to some men when I spotted a tall, thin, good looking gentleman with grey hair, standing in a corner across the room. My friend suggested I go over and introduce myself, so I did. I asked him, “Are you waiting for someone?” He replied, “Yes, I am waiting for a woman to arrive to give me a ticket to a show, then I am leaving.” “Ok,” I said, “I will be sitting at the far table if you have an interest.” Just my luck, a few minutes later, a woman had latched onto him, and she was not the one he was waiting for. They talked and danced for the rest of the evening and then she left. I was surprised, when he walked over to my table and asked me for my social card.

A week later he called and asked me out for dinner. He told me that the woman with the ticket never showed up. It was meant to be, she was the catalyst for the two of us to meet that night.

I knew I had met my twin flame when he mentioned, that, "He was a snowbird and spends the summers at his lake house in New York." Also, he had the striking blue eyes, the physique, and other traits that were in my *Letter of Intention.* Before we met, I had visualized the two of us walking hand in hand by a lake, and it manifested exactly as I had wanted.

The first summer, after our relationship began, he invited me to his lake house and I was very surprised to see more than I had expected. It had three levels with decks, glass windows overlooking the water and majestic mountains, as well as a swimming pool. I felt so grateful and thanked God for giving me my *divine gifts* .

Sale of The Lake House – When the real estate was hot, it was time to sell the lake house and move to something that did not require so much maintenance. Being a special, unique home, the lake house needed a family with teenagers who would enjoy the spiral stairs, the basement apartment and the pool. I bought a little Saint Joseph statue, said the required prayer for a quick sale and buried it in the front yard. A few weeks later, a family with three teenage children had been looking for a lake house and bought it.

Because we needed a new place to live, I began the Law of Attraction process for the perfect townhouse to move into before we left for Florida. I wrote out my *Letter of Intention,* describing everything that we wanted: The location in the same town, move in condition, 2,000 square feet, end unit with views of the Hudson Valley, a fireplace, big kitchen with stainless steel appliances and granite counters, two bedrooms, two bathrooms, finished open basement, outside patio, two balconies, a garage and within our price range

While I was looking on the internet at the real estate townhouses for sale, I noticed a beautiful 2,000 square foot, 2 bedrooms, 3 bath end unit that had just been listed. It was everything I just described with brand new furniture the owners were selling. It was freshly painted, beautifully decorated and even had crown moldings. They accepted our offer, we moved in by the 15th of October, and left for Florida a few weeks later. It was perfect timing. When I looked closely at all the pictures of the townhouse I was surprised to see a small, angel statue on the master bedroom balcony. When we moved in the angel statue was gone!

We spend our summers in New York and our winters in The Villages, Florida. We play golf, go to shows, dance, dine out and socialize with wonderful friends and family. We have been on many cruises to Europe, Mexico and the Caribbean Islands. A few years ago, we flew to London to see the Rolling Stones in concert and toured the English countryside. All these wonderful manifestations came to fruition just as I had asked for in my *Letter of Intention.*

Air Conditioner – A few weeks before leaving for New York I heard my *Inner Guidance System* giving me a message, "Have the air conditioner serviced." I ignored it and the day before I was to leave it stopped working. The temperature in the house was 85 degrees and I frantically called every air conditioner repairman in the phone book. I finally located one who fixed the problem before I left the next day. Thank goodness for my *Inner Guidance System* alerting me. I would have come home at the end of the summer to a disaster due to problems with mold!

Real Estate Transactions – Eight years ago I had invested in a villa to rent out to retired seniors in The Villages. I had some wonderful renters and when the last couple moved out it was time to sell. I visualized a cash buyer who could close quickly so, I buried a Saint Joseph statue under the front window and said the required prayer. Within a few days I got a cash offer. Two weeks later, I closed on the villa and left for New York. It was a lot to do in a short time but it all worked out as I had visualized and wrote in my *Letter of Inten*tion.

Buying A Car – I was interested in buying a Hyundai, Elantra and it had to be a nearly new, preowned vehicle with low miles, white color with beige interior and a moon roof. I looked on line and saw a picture of the exact car I had wanted. The dealership was a half hour away and I was not in the mood to drive there and negotiate the sale with many salesmen. So, I called and asked if they would drive the car to my villa in The Villages. The sales manager agreed and a short time later the car arrived in my driveway. It had only been driven 600 miles and when I took it for a test drive it still had the new car smell.

The car had just become available because the past owner had traded it in for a bigger model. If my *Inner Guidance System* hadn't alerted me to look on line that day, the car would have been sold quickly to someone else. I told the manager that I wanted to buy it but that someone had to drive it back to my house. She agreed to do exactly that and the papers were signed at my dining room table. I handed her a check and the keys to my trade-in with no problems or hassles. The deal was done my way and I bought the exact car I had visualized.

Dog Portrait – While walking my dog I noticed that one of the local stores was having a sale. I went in to look around and saw a beautiful pillow with a picture of a white dog on both sides. I thought to myself, I would love to have an item with my dog's picture. As I walked along the sale table my mouth dropped open. I saw a large bag on a hook with the exact picture of my dog's face on both sides, and the background of the bag was my favorite leopard print. It was a "WOW" moment as I took it off the hook and bought the bag. It just proves that some Law of Attraction items can manifest within minutes.

Wide Brim Sun Hat – I had some minor facial surgery and had to wear a wide brim hat to protect my sensitive skin from the sun. I thought about where I was going to buy this hat but first, before I went shopping, I got a foot message. As I was paying for the massage, a man behind the counter showed me a wide brim hat with my favorite leopard print ribbon. He said, "Would you like this hat?" "Yes," I replied. I looked it over and it was brand new and better yet, he gave it to me for free! How did the hat, that I had visualized, manifest at the foot massage place? Amazing!

Visor – I forgot my tennis visor to shade my eyes from the glaring, hot sun. While I was driving up the long driveway to the tennis courts, I was wondering if I should buy a new visor when, I spotted something white in the middle of the road. There were no other cars in back of me so I stopped and got out to take a closer look. To my surprise, it was a white tennis visor and it looked like it had never been worn. If it was on the grass or on the other side of the street I would have never seen it. No one had claimed the visor at the tennis shop and I was grateful I had a new visor to wear that day.

Positive Affirmations

- I attract all good things into my life.
- I trust the universe to give me abundance of all that I desire.
- I think positive and positive things will happen in my life.
- I choose abundance, happiness, and success in my life.
- My future begins with my next thought.
- Where my attention goes my energy flows.
- I act as though I already have what I desire.
- Whatever I think I can or can't do, I am right.
- I am grateful for what I have.

- The secret is that if I feel I have it all I believe I already do.

- My thoughts become things that manifest into my life.

- What I feel now is what I am going to attract into my life.

- Life is like an echo, what I think about will be returned back to me.

- I am the master of my own destiny and I can make my life what I want it to be.

- I think about only the positive desires I want to manifest in my life.

An Ode to My Twin Flame

By Anne Lauren

From the universal source you came, my one and only twin flame.

Most of our incarnations we have been apart but, you were always there residing in my heart.

I kept praying and asking God what I should do? I knew my desire for you would someday come true.

"Be patient", a small, still voice did say, "You will definitely meet him on that special day. When you have awakened to who you really are, I promise he won't be very far."

I gave a sigh when I received the message from on high. "The time has finally come, tonight you will meet your long, awaited, special guy. You must go to the local, hotel dance and wear your fancy pants."

At the dance he appeared across the room. A great looking guy that I saw out of the corner of my eye. I recognized him right away, with a head of grey hair, eyes of blue and very handsome too! He was my twin flame, I couldn't deny. So, I walked over to him and said, "hi."

When he asked me for my social card later that night, it felt so right.

The next week he called and asked me out on a date, it was definitely fate, now he is my mate.

Many years have passed by and we have had a whole lot of fun with all we have done. Traveling on cruises, European tours, and trips here and there, enjoying our senior years without a care.

No longer will I pine, I thank God and the universe for a perfect find!

Postscript

Congratulations! You now have completed the journey down the road of enlightenment. You have been given the answers and knowledge on how to raise your vibrational frequency from 3D to 5D in order be happy and manifest all your *divine gifts.*

No longer will you feel life is a one-way street, meandering from here to there. You now have a new road map with a destination to love, joy and happiness possibly meeting a loving, romantic, soulmate or your twin flame.

Get out of bed each morning with a spring in your step. Live each day being thankful and grateful for all the universe has given you, and will continue to give you as your life unfolds with all you are asking for.

Don't be concerned what others might say about The Law of Attraction being just a "crazy belief". When they see you have changed your life for the better, are happier, more loving and excited about all your *divine gifts*, they will also want a "piece of the pie."

If everyone used the Law of Attraction *Principles, Processes and Components* in their lives, what a wonderful world it would be!

I wish you the best, and may you always have many "WOW" moments!

BE HAPPY, LIVE, LAUGH AND LOVE ALWAYS,

ANNE LAUREN

Movies, Books, Videos

Law of Attraction Movies: The following movies are twin flame love stories. After you watch each one you will feel a sense of awe as the story brings the twin flames together in very unusual circumstances. I have listed only a few and you can find more on the internet under twin flame movies:

The Notebook (2004) A young couple fall in love, then separate due to the realities of their social status. They have a very powerful love for each other and later reunite in their golden years at a retirement home, realizing they have known each other before. There is a surprise ending

Somewhere in Time (1980) A young man is given a pocket watch by an old woman and finds her again in another lifetime, through unusual circumstances. They are very much in love as young adults only to have it end when he returns back to the present time.

What Dreams May Come (1998) Death brings twin flames together in the afterlife but, he is in heaven and she is in hell. He is determined to reunite with her and he goes through many difficult situations until they are finally reunited. They promise each other when they are reborn again, they will meet as children and start another life together.

Message in a Bottle (1999) A woman finds a love letter in a bottle while walking along the beach. The author is tracked down by the woman, and they fall passionately in love although there are many obstacles that prevent them from ever uniting again.

The Best of Me (2014) High school sweethearts find each other after 20 years apart. An epic love story that captures enduring power of true love lost and then found again.

I Remember You (2015) A love story about two strangers who find love after experiencing a life changing accident. They are soon haunted by an overwhelming sense that they met before in another lifetime.

The Lake House **(**2006) Two people fall in love in different time frames. They communicate by letter sent years apart.

The Last Letter From Your Lover **(**2021) An unhappy married women falls in love with her twin flame but cannot leave her husband. Due to some unfortunate situations, they finally meet again in their senior years.

Brokeback Mountain **(**2005) Two cowboys work together on a sheep farm. They develop an intimate relationship that becomes a profound, eternal, soulmate bond they cannot break. Beautiful mountain backdrop and very intense.

The Secret (2006) Law of Attraction, spiritual documentary.

Law of Attraction Books:

The following are books that will dive deeper into visualization, spirituality, twin flame and soulmates relationships:

Creative Visualization – by Shakti Gawain (1982 New World Library) A technique of using your imagination to create what you want

The Secret – by Rhonda Bryne (2006 Simon and Schuster) The Law of Attraction

The Soulmate Secret – by Arielle Ford, (2006 Collins Publications) Manifest the love of your life with The Law of Attraction.

Divine Love – by Ingrid Darrah, (2014 Balboa Press) From Soulmate Lessons To Twin Flame Reunion.

Twin Souls, Finding Your Spiritual Partner – by Patricia Joudry and Maurie D. Pressman, M.D., (1995 Hazelden Publishing) Finding Your True Spiritual Partner

YouTube Videos:

There are many videos on the internet that will explain The Law of Attraction, here are a few:

How to Create a Vision Board and How it works, by Jack Canfield.

How water and sound affect the body with molecules experiments by the scientist Dr Masaru Emoto

Resources And References

"Ask and You Shall Receive:" Whatever you ask in prayer, believe that you have received it and it will be yours. King James Bible Mark 11:24

The Art of Loving by psychologist Eric Fromm

"Like Attracts Like" – Richard Bach. Things with similar energy level are drawn to each other. The Law of Attraction

"Every reaction has an equal reaction" By Sir Issac Newton's Third Law of Motion

"What Comes Around Goes Around" – Karma Quote

A Course in Miracles – By Helen Schuman Published by The Foundation of Inner Peace and Happiness 1976

The Secret – Movie, The Law of Attraction - By Rhonda Byrne

The Soulmate Secret – By Arielle Ford Balboa Press 2015

Symposium Aristophanes – Plato

Love and Sexuality Part One - Omarah Mikhael Alvanhow – Editions Piosueth 3rd edition 2013.

About the Author

Anne was born in Lake Placid, New York and moved with her family to California when she was three years old. She grew up in Westwood, attended UCLA and became an obstetric nurse. Later, she changed her career to the stock brokerage and real estate business for a more exciting and lucrative job. Her writing career began fifteen years ago when her family went on a RV camping trip that turned out to be a "trip from hell" and a comedy of errors. She felt the vacation disaster would be a great movie and wrote it in screenplay form.

The screenplay took two years to complete and she entered it into a screenwriter's competition for Florida. But, for some unforeseen circumstances, the competition was cancelled. Anne was not going to trash her hard work so, with the advice of a friend, she sent it to a producer in Hollywood. Five years later the screenplay was made into a movie with no credits to her name. What she realizes now is that she needed a movie agent to protect her rights to her script. She plans to make the screenplay into a novel in the near future.

A few years ago, Anne published a memoir about her mother entitled, *Age 101 and Still Having Fun.* Her mother was born in 1902 and passed away in 2004. At 100 years old she was still healthy and lucid when she dictated to Anne, all the details about her long, interesting life. It was displayed in a local bookstore and chosen as “The Book of The Month”. The memoir was also featured in the Villages magazine. You can buy it on Amazon and Barnes and Nobel.

Anne lives in The Villages, Florida with her twin flame and her mini, long haired dachshund. She is very active playing tennis, golf, Mahjongg, Canasta, writing books and running The Dachshund Club. She has two children and five grandchildren.

Anne can be contacted at
TheDivineWay11.11@gmail.com

Made in the USA
Columbia, SC
29 November 2022

72148916R00089